THE ULTIMATE

GUIDE TO NAUTICAL KNOTS

Illustrated by Michel Diament
Translated by Andrea Jones Berasaluce

Skyhorse Publishing

TABLE OF CONTENTS

VOCAB-ULARY

The word "**rope**" is the generic term for any line on a boat. Yet the words "rope" and "line" are almost never used.

Each rope has its own name, according to its place and purpose on board. A "mooring" or a "hawser" serve to moor the boat, and a "halyard" is for raising a sail. A "sheet" adjusts the sail angle. On the boom you'll find the "topping lifts" and the "boom vang."

When making a knot, we distinguish between "**running**" and "**standing**." Running refers to the part of the rope you manipulate to tie the knot, and standing refers to the part that remains unmoving.

By folding a rope in two, you form a **bight**.

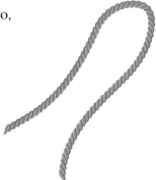

If the strands cross, it becomes a **loop**.

Below are the basic forms:

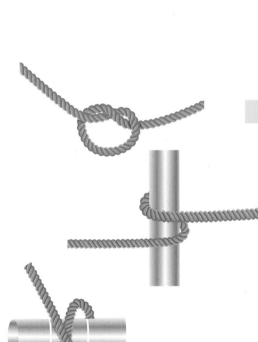

• Simple knot.

• Round turn, which refers to wrapping the line around a support.

• Half hitch, which refers to wrapping the line around a support with its strands crossing.

KNOTS

BOWLINE

This is a classic nautical knot with
multiple uses. It is solid and
does not slip, but nevertheless,
it's easy to tie and untie.

STEP 1
Make a loop.

STEP 2
Pass the running end (or running part) through the loop.

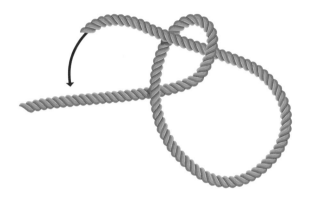

STEP 3
The running end goes around the standing end (or standing part) and then back through the loop. To tighten the knot, pull the standing end and the running end at the same time.

VARIATION
BOWLINE BEND

Using two bowlines, you can make a bowline bend—a handy way of connecting two ropes, especially if they have different diameters!

RUNNING BOWLINE

The running bowline is very useful for making a sliding loop, which is often used to tie a vessel to a mooring buoy.

STEP 1
Fold the rope to make a bight. Form a loop along the left strand and pass the running end over the standing end.

STEP 2

Take the running end, pass it behind the standing end, and then through the loop you made in the beginning. Finish by going back though the large loop from behind, then through the small one.

STEP 3

The knot is finished.

FIGURE EIGHT KNOT

This very simple stopper knot, among other things, prevents a rope from "escaping" a pulley. In general, it's advisable to tie this knot well above the end of the rope (at least 8 inches [20 cm] up).

STEP 1
Make a loop.

STEP 2

Pass the running end under the standing end, then through the loop. When going through the loop, first go through the top part and then through the bottom.

STEP 3

Pull the ends to tighten.

CLOVE HITCH

The clove hitch, a classic of the mooring hitches, is particularly simple to tie. It's very useful for keeping a fender in place.

STEP 1
Wrap once around a support.

STEP 2

Take the running end and wrap the rope a second time around the support next to the first wrap, going back to front, and slide the running end beneath.

STEP 3

Tighten firmly.

ROUND TURN AND TWO HALF HITCHES

This is the ultimate mooring hitch. It's a straightforward hitch, quick to tie and untie, and also has multiple uses.

STEP 1
Make two round turns around a support.

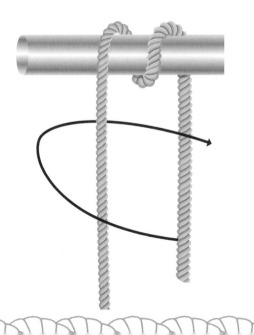

STEP 2

With the running end, make a loop that passes first in front of, then in back of, the standing end.

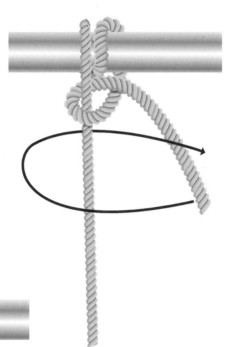

STEP 3

Make a second loop with the running end, turning it in the same direction as the first. Finish the hitch by pulling the running end to raise the loops.

CLEAT HITCH

No great mystery as to its use: this knot
securely attaches a line to a cleat.
To practice tying this knot,
you can use a doorknob or a
piece of furniture.

STEP 1
Wrap the rope around the cleat
from bottom to top, bring the
line back in front of the cleat,
and start wrapping it again.

STEP 2
Make a loop along the running end.

STEP 3
Thread the loop onto the cleat without turning it over.

ROLLING HITCH

The rolling hitch is generally used to
connect a finer tether to a thicker,
very taut rope. Therefore, by pulling
on a taut rope, you can offset its tension by
allowing it to recover some slack,
even releasing when stuck.
By the way, you can also use the
rolling hitch to hang a hammock!

STEP 1
Make a hitch. Note: in
a real-life situation,
it will be necessary to
make sure to wrap in the
right direction in order
to be able to pull the rope.

STEP 2
With the running end, make a loop above the round turn.

STEP 3
Pull the two strands to tighten the hitch.

OVERHAND LOOP

This is an easy knot to tie; however,
once tightened, it is very difficult to undo.
It can be made right in the middle of a rope.
The overhand loop allows for isolating
a damaged part of a rope or simply
making a loop.

STEP 1
Make a bight along the
rope and fold the rope
in two, raising the
bight upward.

STEP 2
Slide the bight behind the standing end to make a simple knot.

STEP 3
Tighten the knot.

THIEF KNOT

The thief knot is easy to undo quickly (thieves used it to swiftly untie the reins of their horses). It is used when a rope must be released rapidly on a sailboat in order, for instance, to hold back the boom, or when it is necessary to have both hands free to work on the boat.

STEP 1
Make a bight along the rope and pass it behind the length of line you want to release.

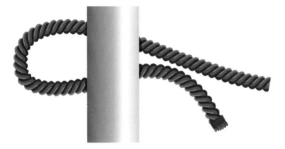

STEP 2
Make a second bight on the free strand of rope, which is on the side that stays tense, and pass it through the first bight.

STEP 3
Make a third bight with the free strand and pass it through the bight made during Step 2.

STEP 4

Tighten by pulling the strand on the tense side.
To undo the knot, just pull the free strand.

HEAVING LINE KNOT

The heaving line knot isn't so easy to achieve, but it holds well even when struck and can also be undone quite easily. It is used as a stopper knot on a rope to keep it from coming off a pulley.

STEP 1

Make a loop at the end of the rope, then take the running end and wrap around the standing end, going over-under, over-under.

STEP 2

With the running end, go back through all the
bights you just made and through the initial loop.

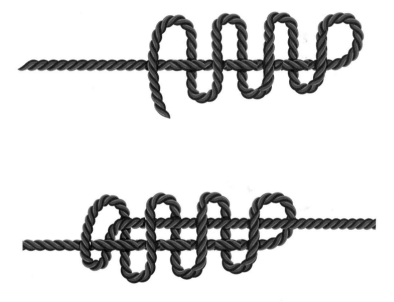

STEP 3
Tighten it all by pulling the two free strands.

WHIPPING KNOT

Once a rope is cut, the strands tend to unravel and the rope gets loose. The whipping knot prevents a line from coming undone. The whipping knot is used on all ropes as soon as they have been cut.

STEP 1

Take the line in which you'll tie the whipping knot. Make a bight—where the curve lies at the very end of the rope. Then turn the line that you'll use to tie the whipping knot up toward the end of the rope, turning it the opposite direction of that in which it is plaited.

STEP 2

The whipping knot should also be as long as the rope is wide and stop ¼ of an inch (½ a centimeter) from the end. The end of the bight should not be covered by the whipping knot. Pass the running end through the bight.

STEP 3

Gently pull to pass the bight and the line through it under the whipping knot. The rope with the whipping knot is cut at a length of 1¼ to 1¾ of an inch (3 to 4 centimeters).

SQUARE KNOT

The square knot serves to hold a folded
sail when not in use. It's important
not to tie this knot wrong, for if a strand
passes over or under incorrectly,
the sail's sure to unfurl!

STEP 1

Make a bight with a rope. With another rope, wrap it first
from beneath, then go above, then slide it under the two
strands of the bight.

STEP 2
Finish by passing it over and under.

STEP 3
Essential: no matter what, if the two strands come out above one side, then they must come out underneath on the other side.
To tighten the knot, pull the four strands at the same time.

REEF KNOT

This is a knot used on the gaskets to reef, or reduce the area of, a sail. It is very similar to the square knot.

STEP 1

Make a bight with one rope, shown here as the blue rope. Using a second rope, make a second bight and pass the strands under and over.

STEP 2

Take the upper strand of the second bight and go under the first bight.

STEP 3

Tighten well for the knot to hold.

SHEET BEND

This is a very old and universal bend. It's used often on board, even if it is not always very solid. It serves to knot together two ropes, even if they have different thicknesses. It's also called the becket bend or weaver's knot.

STEP 1
Make a bight with the first rope, shown here in yellow. Using a second rope, pass it under the bight and then behind the two strands.

STEP 2

Finish by forming a loop with the running end that passes under itself. There should be a strand of the running end that comes out below the standing end, while the other strand comes out above the standing end. Gently pull the four strands to tighten the knot.

DOUBLE SHEET BEND

It is more resistant than the simple sheet bend, and it's especially used in fishing.

STEP 1

Make a bight with the first rope. Then pass a second rope under the bight, over the top strand, then under both strands at the same time.

STEP 2

Take the second rope and make a loop around the knotting by first passing it in front of the group of strands and then behind the group of strands. Once finished, the running end then passes over the initial bight, under itself, and again over the bight.

STEP 3

Gently pull the four strands at the same time to tighten the knot.

CARRICK BEND

This is a bend that holds very well, yet remains easy to undo. It is also very decorative!

STEP 1

Make a loop with the first rope. Take a second rope and place it on the loop. Then pass it under the first strand and over the second. Continue making the knot passing the rope under, over, under.

STEP 2

It results in this, which, when not tightened all the way, has a very decorative effect.

STEP 3

You can also tighten the knot by pulling the strands.

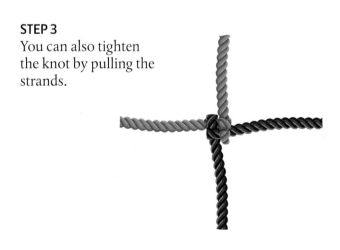

FISHERMAN'S KNOT

Commonly used in fishing, it primarily serves to connect two ropes, even if they have different diameters. Attention: This knot, when tight or doubled, can be particularly difficult to untie.

STEP 1
Make a simple knot with the end of one rope around another rope.

STEP 2

Take the end of the rope around the one you just made a knot on and make another simple knot. Firmly tighten both knots.

STEP 3

To tighten the whole thing and finish the knot, pull the two standing ends at the same time.

ANCHOR BEND

This is also called the fisherman's bend. You can use it to connect something to a ring. It is particularly effective if the ropes are wet or slippery.

STEP 1
Make a round turn around the ring.

STEP 2
Pass the running end above the standing end and then put it through the inside of the round turn.

STEP 3
Make a half hitch using the free strand.

STEP 4
Tighten securely.

ANGLER'S LOOP

This knot is also known as the perfection loop. It lets you make a very solid fixed loop. It's particularly recommended for use on synthetic or slippery ropes.

STEP 1
Start by making a loop. With the running end, go back up to make a second loop above the first.

STEP 2
Pass the running
end under the
standing end.

STEP 3

Go back up with the running end and pass it between the two loops, then take the bight as shown in the illustration and pass it through the inside of the first loop.

STEP 4

To finish the knot, pull alternately on the bight that has been slid through and on the two strands, taking care to maintain the knot's position.

COIL

On a boat, there can never be ropes
that "hang down/drag" or get tangled or
damaged because they are improperly stored.
There are, therefore, solutions to keeping
the ropes in order. The coil is one of these.
Technically speaking, ropes are "coiled"
or "wound." There are all kinds of coils.

STEP 1

Fold the rope in two. Let the bight hang by holding the other end, and begin wrapping it to coil the rope. It's essential to wrap evenly. The rope should not look like a "figure eight" when wound.

When the entire rope is wound, encircle the coil with the bight and put it back through the upper part.

STEP 2
The bight can then be used to hang
the coiled rope.

MONKEY'S FIST

**At its core, this knot serves as "ballast"
for a rope so that it can be thrown.
It's a very popular decorative knot.**

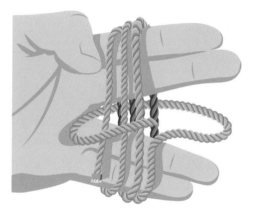

STEP 1
Take a rope, wrap it three times
vertically around your fingers.
Once the running end is back in
your palm, wrap it three times
horizontally to encircle all the
strands.

STEP 2
Once the running end is back in your palm after the third horizontal wrap, slide it between the vertical strands and your fingers, then carefully slide the knotting to lift it off your hand.

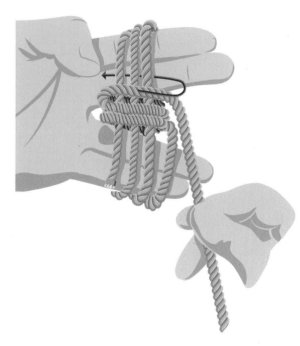

STEP 3

Holding the knotting securely so that it does not come undone, circle the horizontal strands three times with the running end.

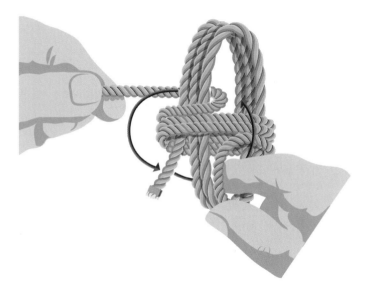

STEP 4

The principle is now set: you keep wrapping three times in one direction, three times in another. With a sufficiently thick rope, you can use the same method, except start by wrapping around four fingers to get a perfect monkey fist. The finer the rope, the more it will be necessary for the monkey fist to be tightened from the outset to produce a harmonious result. For instance, you could start tying the knot around two fingers.

Direction: Guillaume Pô
Editorial Direction: Elisabeth Pegeon
Editing: Julie Quillien
Artistic Direction: Isabelle Mayer
Page Layout: Catherine Enault
Illustrations: Michel Diament
Production Management: Thierry Dubus
Manufacturing Monitoring: Marie Guibert
Proofreading (French edition): Alain Tardif
Translation: Andrea Jones Berasaluce

Skyhorse Publishing books may be purchased in bulk at special discounts for
sales promotion, corporate gifts, fund-raising, or educational purposes. Special
editions can also be created to specifications. For details, contact the Special Sales
Department, Skyhorse Publishing, 307 West 36th Street, 11th Floor, New York, NY
10018 or info@skyhorsepublishing.com.

Skyhorse® and Skyhorse Publishing® are registered trademarks of
Skyhorse Publishing, Inc.®, a Delaware corporation.

Visit our website at www.skyhorsepublishing.com.

10 9 8 7 6 5 4 3 2 1

Library of Congress Cataloging-in-Publication Data is available on file.

Cover design by Kai Texel
Cover Image: Getty Images

Print ISBN: 978-1-5107-5927-5
Ebook ISBN: 978-1-5107-5928-2

Printed in China